This book belongs

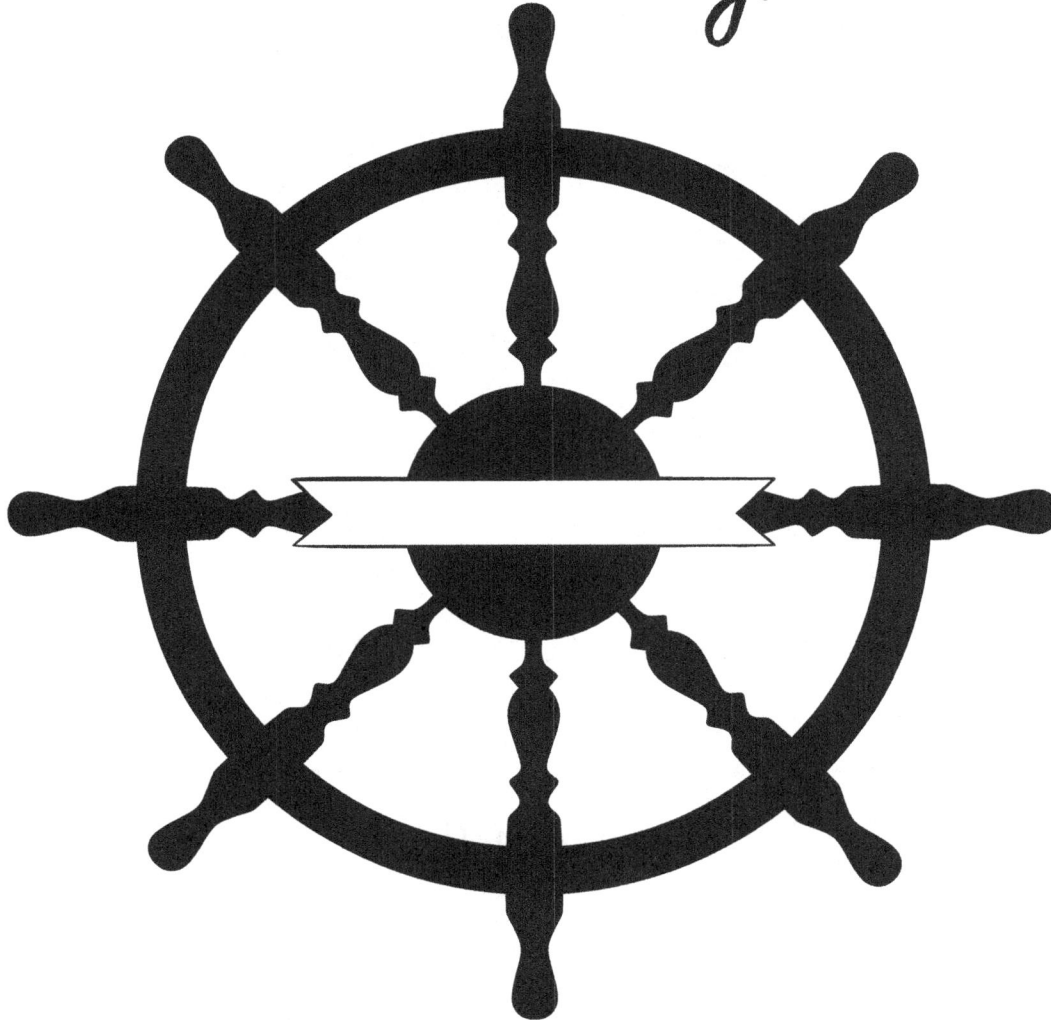

This book may not be reproduced or transmitted in any form or
by any means, electronic or mechanical without
written permission from the publisher. Permission is granted to
photocopy individual pages for personal, noncommercial use by
the purchaser.

Some images courtesy of
www.vecteezy.com/free-vector/collection

Christian coloring for Seniors

People, Places & Things!

50 unique designs which will appeal to men but are suitable for anyone! With **Scripture verses on God's faithfulness, family and love**

With a blank page after every design to allow for bleed thru. So you can use markers, pencils, crayons or any medium you like!

. . . .

As you relax and color, may the word of God be a blessing to you!

. . . .

Sarah J. Stuart

sarahjstuartpublishing@gmail.com

So be strong and courageous! Do not be afraid and do not panic before them. For the Lord your God will personally go ahead of you. He will neither fail you nor abandon you."
Deuteronomy 31:6

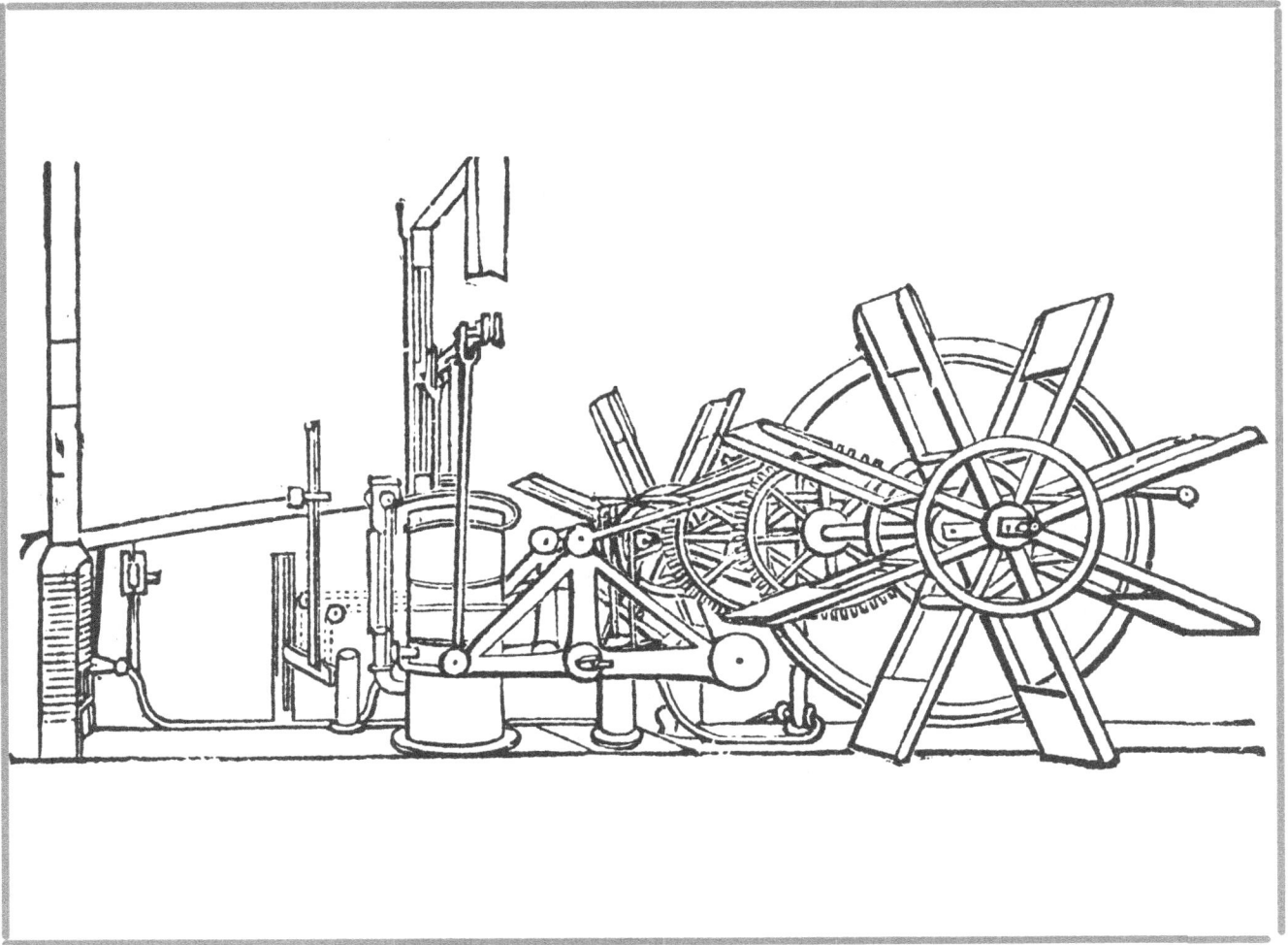

For the Lord your God is the supreme God of the heavens above and the earth below.

Joshua 2:11

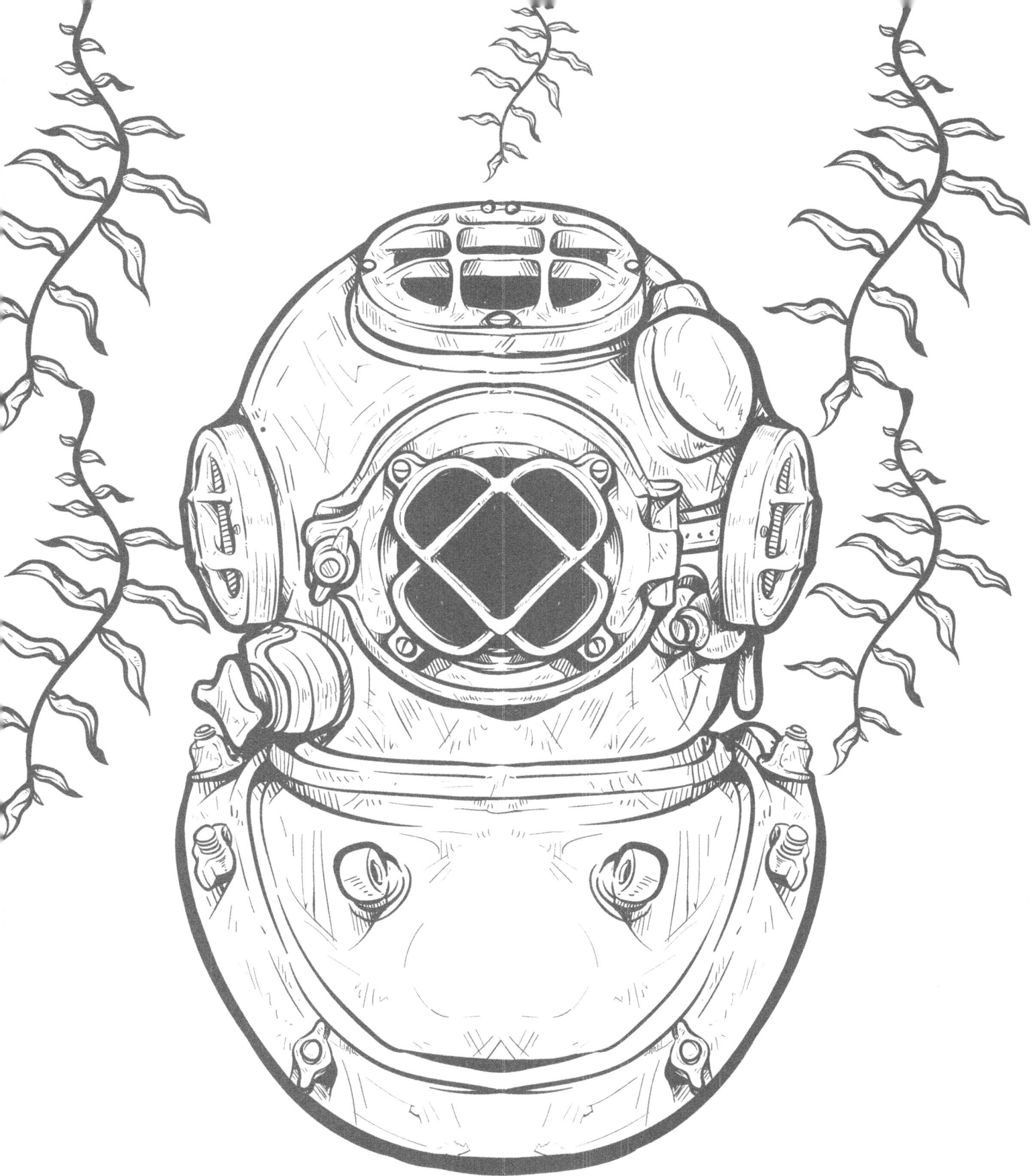

March on with courage, my soul!

Judges 5:21

Take courage and be a man.

1 Kings 2:2

Take courage as you fulfill your duties, and may the Lord be with those who do what is right.

2 Chronicles 19:11

Having hope will give you courage. You will be protected and will rest in safety.

Job 11:18

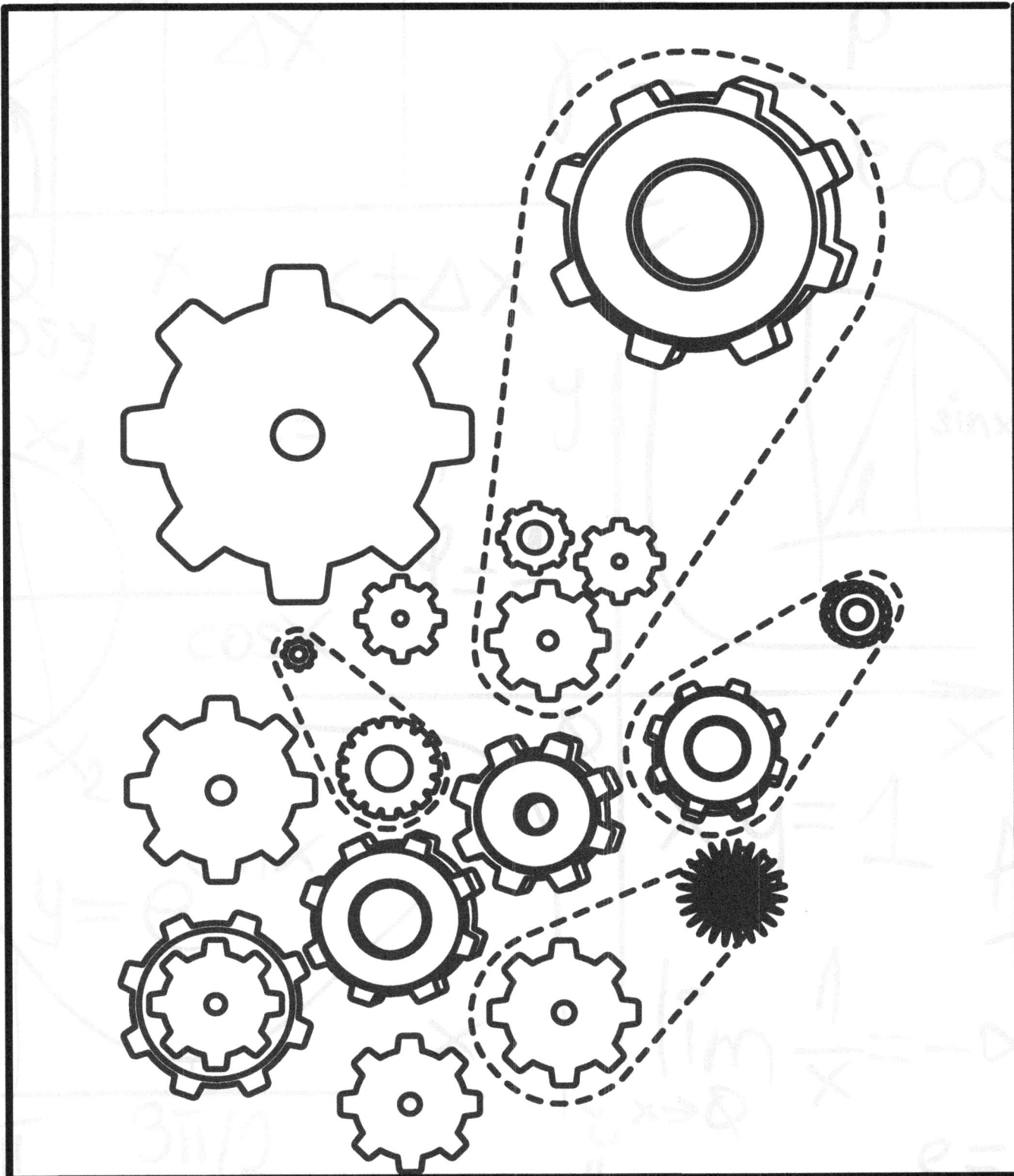

WAIT PATIENTLY FOR THE LORD.

Psalm 27:14

BE ON GUARD. STAND FIRM IN THE FAITH.

1 Corinthians 16:13

But Christ, as the Son, is in charge of God's entire house.

Hebrews 3:6

TAKE COURAGE, FOR THE COMING OF THE LORD IS NEAR. James 5:8

He is the Rock;
his deeds are
perfect. Deuteronomy
32:4

He is a
faithful God
who does no
wrong.

Deuteronomy 32:4

You are faithful to your promises, O my God.

Psalm 71:22 part

The ends of the earth
have seen the victory of
our God. Psalm 98:3

For the Lord is a faithful God. Blessed are those who wait for his help.

Isaiah 30:18

He is faithful to do what He says

1 Corinthians 1:9 part

The temptations in your life are no different from what others experience. And God is faithful. He will not allow the temptation to be more than you can stand.

1 Corinthians 10:13

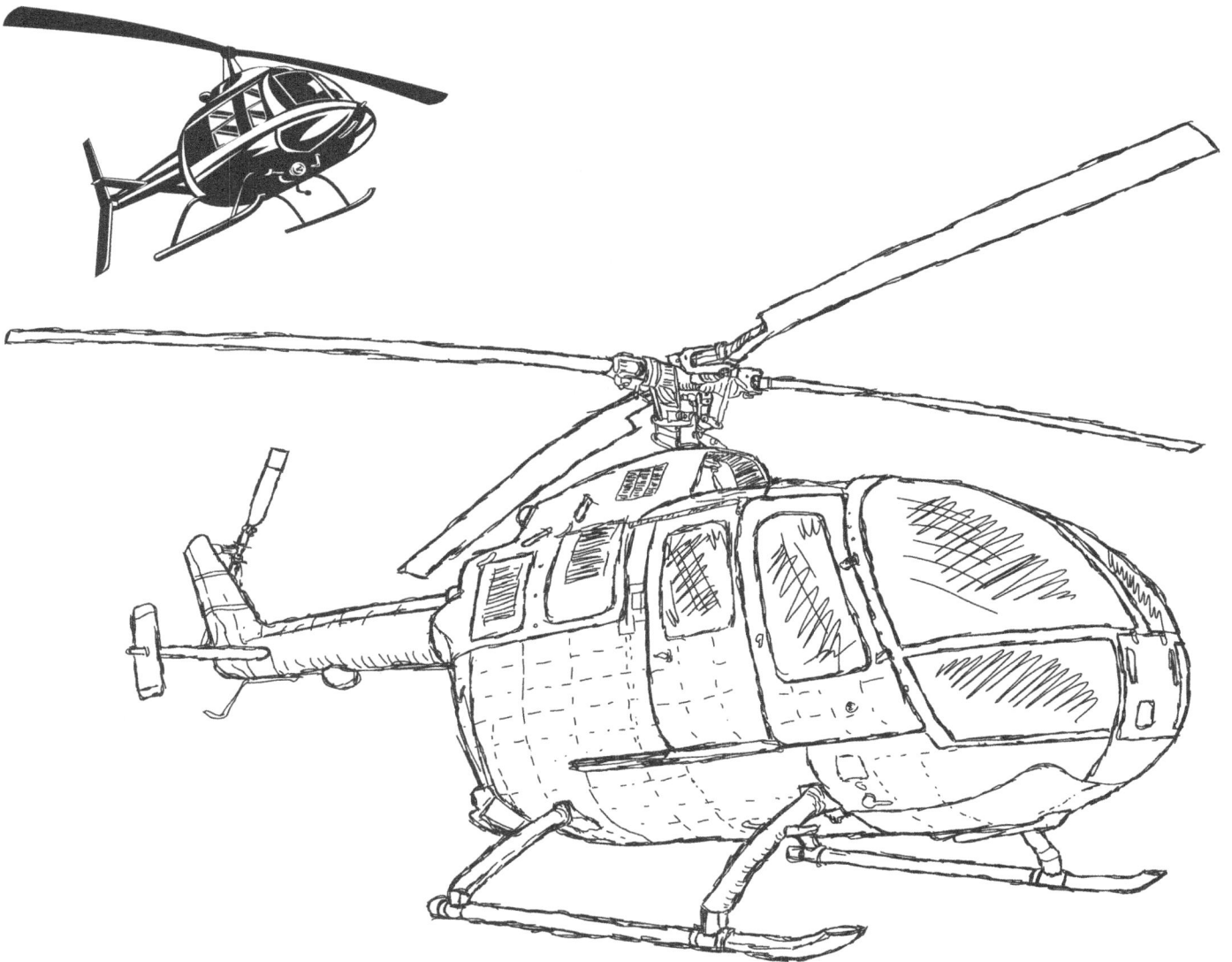

WE FAITHFULLY PREACH THE TRUTH.
GOD'S POWER IS WORKING IN US

2 CORINTHIANS 6:7

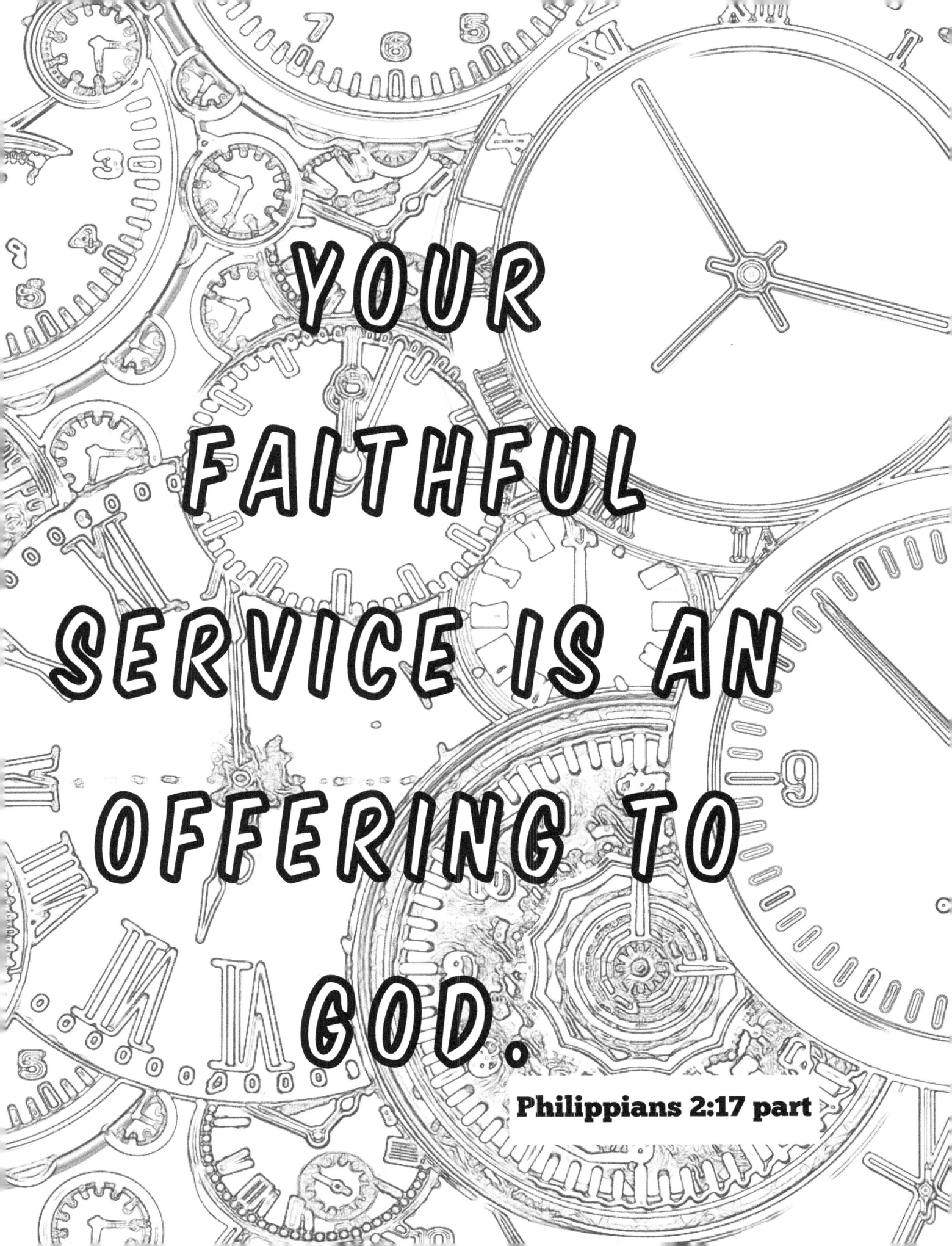

YOUR FAITHFUL SERVICE IS AN OFFERING TO GOD.

Philippians 2:17 part

"I am El-Shaddai —'God Almighty.' Serve me faithfully and live a blameless life."

Genesis 17:1

You are faithful to your promises, O my God.

Psalm 71:22

I listen carefully to what God the Lord is saying, for He speaks peace to His faithful people. Psalm 85:8

You are
entirely
faithful.

Psalm 89:8 part

THE ENDS OF
THE EARTH
HAVE SEEN
THE VICTORY
OF OUR GOD.

Psalm 98:3

Blessed are those
who wait for His help.

Isaiah 30:18 part

MAY THOSE WHO LOVE YOUR SALVATION REPEATEDLY SHOUT, "GOD IS GREAT!"

PSALM 70:4 PART

God gives rest to his loved ones. Psalm 127:2

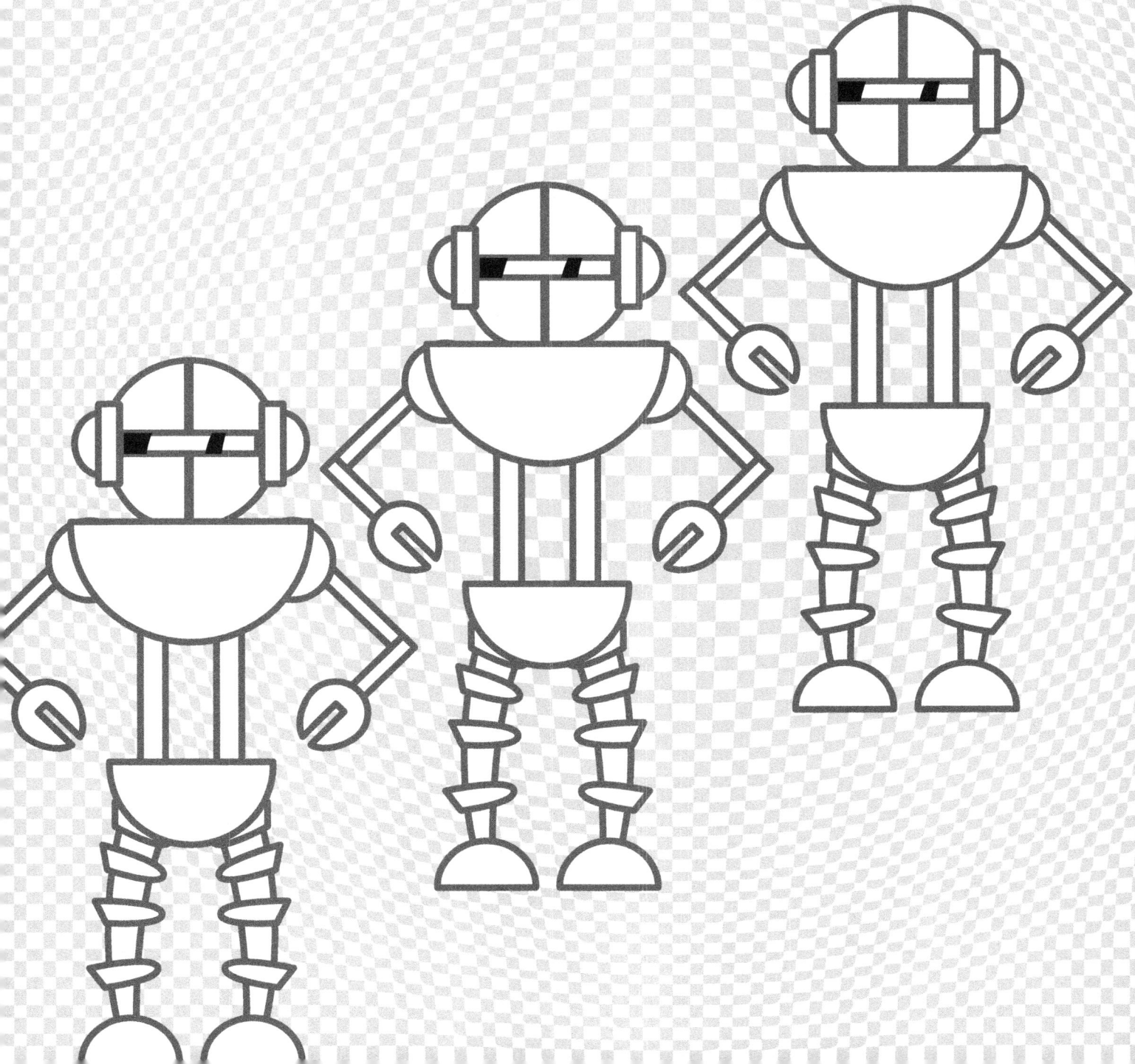

Hate evil and love what is good

Amos 5:15 part

O PEOPLE, THE LORD HAS TOLD YOU
WHAT IS GOOD, AND THIS IS WHAT HE
REQUIRES OF YOU: TO DO WHAT IS
RIGHT, TO LOVE MERCY, AND TO WALK
HUMBLY WITH YOUR GOD.

MICAH 6:8

"For the Lord your God is living among you. He is a mighty savior. He will take delight in you with gladness. With his love, he will calm all your fears. He will rejoice over you with joyful songs." Zephaniah 3:17

"FOR THIS IS HOW GOD LOVED THE WORLD: HE GAVE HIS ONE AND ONLY SON, SO THAT EVERYONE WHO BELIEVES IN HIM WILL NOT PERISH BUT HAVE ETERNAL LIFE."

John 3:16

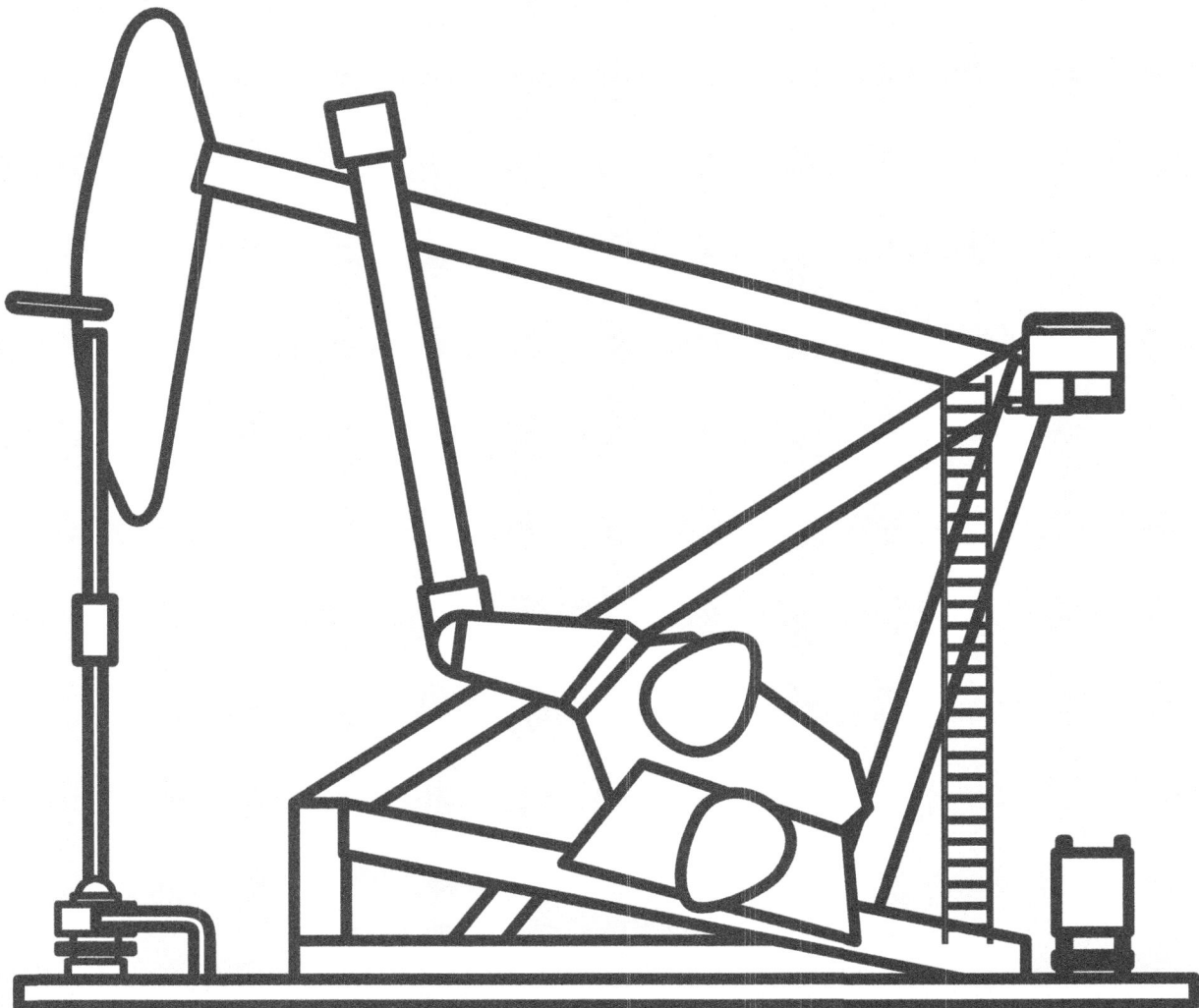

If God is for us, who can ever be against us?

Romans 8:31 part

"NO EYE HAS SEEN, NO EAR HAS HEARD, AND NO MIND HAS IMAGINED WHAT GOD HAS PREPARED FOR THOSE WHO LOVE HIM."

1 Corinthians 2:9

IT IS NO LONGER I WHO LIVE, BUT CHRIST LIVES IN ME.

GALATIANS 2:20 PART

BUT GOD IS SO RICH IN
MERCY, AND HE LOVED
US SO MUCH
EPHESIANS 2:4

AND MAY YOU HAVE THE POWER TO UNDERSTAND, AS ALL GOD'S PEOPLE SHOULD, HOW WIDE, HOW LONG, HOW HIGH, AND HOW DEEP HIS LOVE IS.

EPHESIANS 3:18

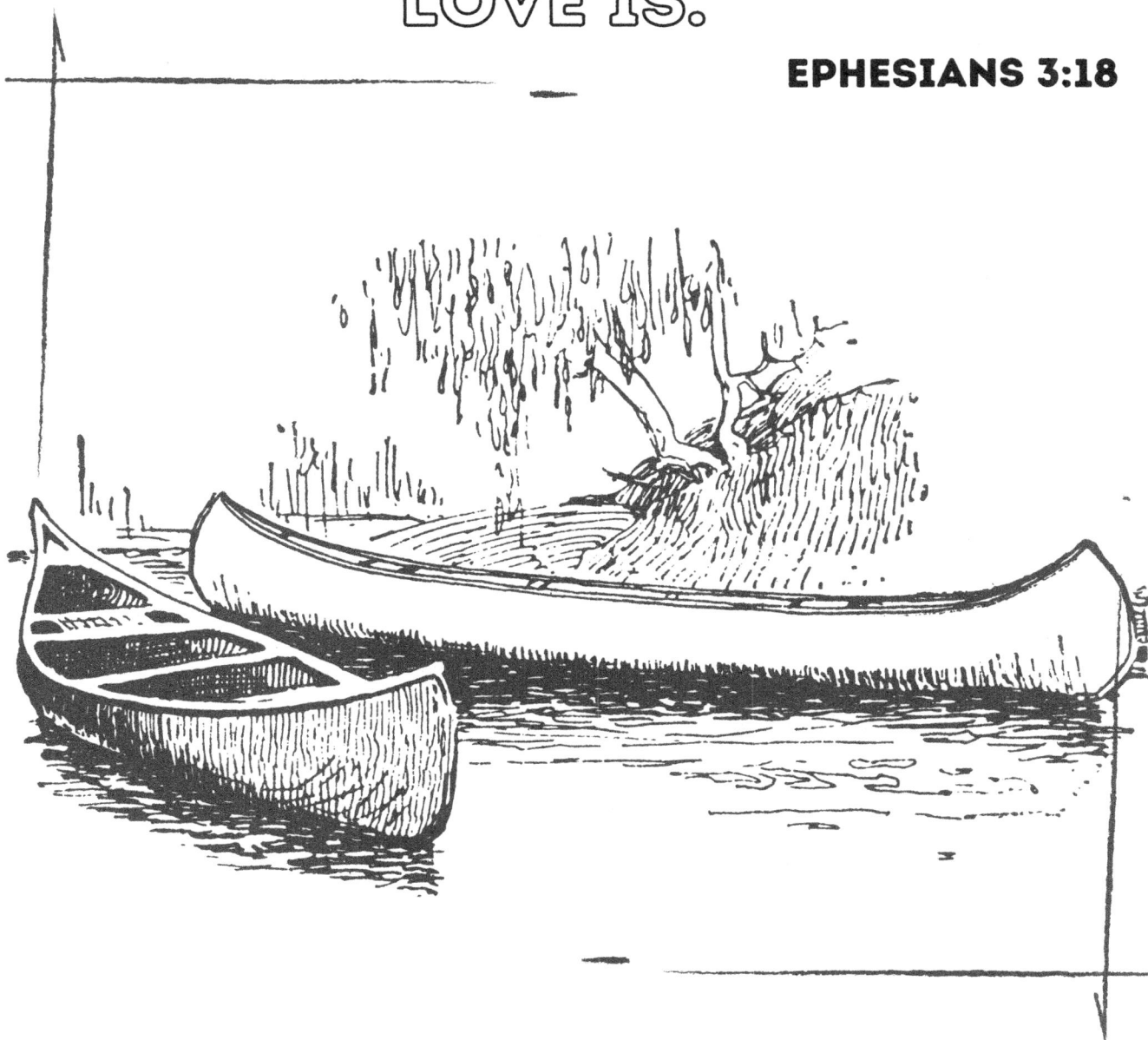

FOR GOD IS NOT UNJUST. HE WILL NOT FORGET HOW HARD YOU HAVE WORKED FOR HIM AND HOW YOU HAVE SHOWN YOUR LOVE TO HIM BY CARING FOR OTHER BELIEVERS, AS YOU STILL DO.

HEBREWS 6:10

BUT THOSE WHO OBEY GOD'S WORD TRULY SHOW HOW COMPLETELY THEY LOVE HIM. THAT IS HOW WE KNOW WE ARE LIVING IN HIM.

1 JOHN 2:5

See how very much our Father loves us, for he calls us his children, and that is what we are!

1 John 3:1 part

Dear friends, let us continue to love one another, for love comes from God.

1 John 4:7 part

Anyone who loves is a child of God and knows God.

1 John 4:7 part

This is real love—not that we loved God, but that he loved us and sent his Son as a sacrifice to take away our sins

1 John 4:10

BUT IF WE LOVE EACH OTHER, GOD LIVES IN US, AND HIS LOVE IS BROUGHT TO FULL EXPRESSION IN US.

1 John 4:12 part

We know how much God loves us, and we have put our trust in His love.

1 John 4:16 part

God is love, and all who live in love live in God, and God lives in them.

1 John 4:16b

Everyone who believes that Jesus is the Christ has become a child of God.

1 John 5:1a

You are citizens along with all of God's holy people. You are members of God's family.

Ephesians 2:19

THIS IS MY COMMAND—BE STRONG AND COURAGEOUS! DO NOT BE AFRAID OR DISCOURAGED. FOR THE LORD YOUR GOD IS WITH YOU WHEREVER YOU GO.

Joshua 1:9

Made in the USA
Las Vegas, NV
20 February 2023

67835353R00057